The Beautiful Noon of No Shadow

The Beautiful Noon of
No
Shadow

Poems by Susan Ludvigson

Louisiana State University Press
Baton Rouge and London   1986

Designer: Laura Roubique
Typeface: Century Old Style
Typesetter: G&S Typesetters, Inc.
Printer: Thomson-Shore, Inc.
Binder: John H. Dekker & Sons, Inc.

10 9 8 7 6 5 4 3 2 1

The author gratefully acknowledges the editors of the following publications, in
which some of the poems herein first appeared: *Antioch Review, Arts Journal,
Caesura, Conversations with South Carolina Poets, From Mt. San Angelo,
Georgia Review, The Made Thing, Michigan Quarterly Review, Missouri Review,
Nation, Poetry, Southern Poetry Review,* and *Verse.*

Library of Congress Cataloging-in-Publication Data

Ludvigson, Susan.
    The beautiful noon of no shadow.

    I. Title.
PS3562.U27B43   1986   811'.54   86-21073
ISBN 0-8071-1378-6
ISBN 0-8071-1379-4 (pbk.)

Contents

Acknowledgments

I would like to express my gratitude to the John Simon
Guggenheim Foundation, the Fulbright Commission (The
Council for International Exchange of Scholars), and the
National Endowment for the Arts for fellowships that made
the writing of this book possible.

I'd also like to thank Harriet Doar, Kathryn Kirkpatrick,
Lynne McMahon, Sherod Santos, Julie Suk, and Beth
Tornes for their generous and valuable criticisms of
poems.

The Beautiful Noon of No Shadow

The Turning

It's like the clarity of fever—
suddenly what you knew
in the space before restless sleep
is alive as the whole past,
trembling, and the future
an arc you've put your right
foot on at the base,
which doesn't give.
You know you can't see
the other side,
with its 16th century houses
half-falling into streams,
the one river
that cuts through a village
you already love.
You have viewed its plain church
and modest lake
just twice, and briefly.
You know the city though,
can remember each bridge,
how sun hits the lamps afternoons
and where dark bronze
casts dozing shadows.

Here is all you have grown
to expect, and the phone
warms your ear,
if not like a lover's breath,
at least with old affection.
You work. You drive a car.
You speak to the doctor
who understands your questions
and with mild eyes answers.
Your mother, your child
gather your words like wildflowers.
But when you disappear
into pages, again and again
your eye lights on the names
that tell you
what you're heading toward,
as if flares had just been lit.

1

1

Even pain you can take, in waves:
Call the interval happiness.

—*William Stafford*

In the Absence of Angels

We want to believe
in the ones who take their children
to the zoo in strollers, murmuring
at lions and giraffes, their faces
lined with patience and sun. We think
they have never known days
when they must identify morning
by the relative lightness of gray,
have never felt autumn
rest on their hearts like fever.
But many, even of these,
must climb long ladders toward dawn.

I remember a decade of dark
when sometimes I walked
as if in the nightmare of chase,
my steps slow, as through deep snow.
Now I see, in child, lover and friend,
the same cellophane look in the eyes,
the same absence of angels,
and I ask again, into afternoon light,
how can we learn to be who we are
in the beautiful noon of no shadow?

The Dream of Birds

Again it was one I forgot
to feed. Sometimes
there are whole cages of finches,
cockatiels, parakeets
living, but barely,
on seed moldy with age,
and no water. This time
it was the peach-faced lovebird
I once let go from his cage
in a climate he might
have survived in. He flew
to sit on the fence and call back,
his shrill chirp bewildered,
angry. At last he went
into a pine and away—
those iridescent tail feathers,
turquoise and green,
I used to collect when they fell
and send in letters to friends—
gone. In the dream
early this morning, it was
that bird. My heart went
dark with remorse. I could feel
the blood filling it, fast,
the way love does, and that regret.

Games of Chance

How often we rediscover it:
the letter unexpectedly overturned
while looking for an address—

or in some innocuous movie,
a comedy, that sudden image
of the self in pajamas
watching adults at a card table,

or the dream where a friend dies,
her ghost crying the fear
that she'll be forgotten, even as
we put our arms around
her still substantial form—

and we know once more how the past
creeps out of its shadow.

It shows us the lover who wrote each week
to tell his sorrows.
He's still behind the same desk,
contemplates the same photographs,
weeps for the life he doesn't have.

And the child who believed that parents
knew how the world was organized,
and how their fires—
toasted marshmallow evenings
and backyard barbeques—
seemed always under control.

And the friend who loses her life
again and again,
our grief the way she knows
what she needs to go on.

When There Is No Surface

When there is no surface to rise through,
when lake and sky lose their separation
as dream and waking sometimes do,

so that the dream dreams emancipation
from itself, and you can wake over and over
inside the dream—then a breathless suspicion

blooms and scatters its strange flowers
through the memory, which wants to know
what it loves, and who he is that towers

above sleep and sleeplessness and grows
even as his absence becomes greater.
Was he a stranger whose affections flowed

into rooms you hadn't guessed? Much later
you think so. But when he is so much
part of you, you cannot believe you were the creator

of this myth, that it was half illusion. Such
love breathed through us, it became the air,
you sigh, grief and conviction mixed, the clutch

at the heart when you cry it bearable
only because you cannot yet concede that perfection
was something else, and is gone. *Unfair,*

you whisper when his friends speak of his defection
and insist they can't imagine anyone so right for him
as you are. You try to see him as the mere projection

of your wishes. But you had those nights, and swim
even now in the streams of that desire,
unable to release the self's dark twin.

The Sudden Approach of Trees

The glittery video flashes
and the scene repeats. Directly
in that line of vision,
I keep driving
fast down the highway,
two cars ahead of me
passing each other wildly
until the collision,
the road going on and on
through flat green fields
toward a bright horizon.

I know this highway.
Soon there'll be
a restaurant on the left,
a dark place, nearly hidden
in trees. Upstairs, a hotel
where a woman stands
in a corridor,
a man she loves in a room
on one side, his son
across the hall, playing
with cards he spreads
on a blanket.
The child is curious, pleased
this stranger has come
to them. The father, nervous,
steps into the corridor once,
brings the woman an apple,
touches her hair.

They hear cars going by
on the highway,
the same sequence of cars,
over and over.
Two pass each other,
just there, before
the dark building.
Each time,
a third one follows,
seeming to slow
at the sudden approach
of these shady trees.

Waiting for Your Life

for Nello

I. Love

This is the child's secret—
the word he hears whispered close
when he's half asleep—
the one parents demand,
and all the cousins.
It means something he can't quite find,
and sometimes nothing at all.
When someone smiles,
breathing it, he sees the slats
of the crib, the way shadows
play on the windows
with only the night-light glowing.
He tries to respond by laughing.
Often, in a corner alone,
he dreams of the shape he thinks
it must have, the colors he almost
imagines, the transparent walls
through which arms reach,
the open mouth that might almost,
he thinks, be crying.

II. Return

Nothing specific comes back at first
except the hollow where sun
streams in, and the sense
that everyone's happy, the fear
that you will never know
what others assume.
Then your hometown in Italy
spreads its morning over
the present. The light, the heat
are forty years old:

A small girl, your age,
is washing her hands
in a fountain, her hair
glistening, damp from the spray.
When you take her hand,
you notice how the water beads
on her braids as on the wings
of blackbirds after rain.
Then you see crystals
like the ones that hang
in your mother's dining room,
spinning the walls to color.

Now your mother calls
from a hill, her voice
barely audible on the wind.
You try to understand
the words, but they
drift away from you,
float past your father who sits
under a tree playing cards,
his friends' laughter
making the air spread out
and ripple above you.
Her voice is lost
in the silvery leaves.
To recover it, you climb
the hill to where she waits,
hands angrily waving.
You follow her home.

You have seen the girl
or someone like her
many times, grown.
But when she appears,
almost as quickly
she disappears
like desire that evaporates
in the smallest breeze.

Today at the flea market
while you buy a lamp,
while you pick up a vase
and examine it, the blue
of the glass in the sun
almost blinding,
your mother sits in a small room,
the heavy red curtains drawn,
her voice rising, then falling
like water, or song
each time she repeats your name.

III. At the Sanitorium

At St. Hilaire du Touvet, you made
a novel in photographs, a *photo-roman—*
cartoon clouds of dialogue, the posed scenes
like stills from a movie, shots of tiaras and capes
brightening the black and white landscape.
Death wore his fatherly face as a mask,
while you, thin sad boy of twenty or so,
disguised yourself, your illness,
behind and before the camera.
One character, Sonia, might have been
one of the dozens of women
who've laid their small hands
in yours and said yes. For two months,
you tell me, killing the time, you and some others
carted equipment, created the story—
Qui es-tu, mon amour?—
half joke and half nightmare, where
love is elusive as light—
as the shadowy outline of you in one frame,
almost lost in an upper corner, more clear
in the next, then gone.

A century ago, instead of this
glossy record, there'd have been drawings—
figures leaner, more pale
as the months progressed.

You spat not blood, but colors
you'd breathed painting scarves,
filmy enchantments you'd sold in cafés.

Now your lungs deny those old assaults,
though a cough remains, and I see it
in the dark, as blue, and then yellow,
leaping from silky flame.

A good time, you say, where rest and ease
produced people who look
as if they were bred for pictures—
not romantics wasting away, but rosy youth
preparing to return to the world.

Your own preparations began and go on.
Now graying and muscular,
you take out the loose-leaf book
where you and the other patients
are ranged against cool mountain sky.
Your princely body restored to health,
you whisper the question again
as if into still thin air.

IV. When Love Becomes

the too-bright flower
of your death opening, you stop,
the image arresting your hands.

I try to imagine those velvety petals, or silk—
the pink lining of coffins, rich invitations
to lie down and down.

Waiting for you to return to your body, and mine,
I suddenly see the diaries
shelved on the walls of your dreams.

Now years are being torn and tossed
out the night window,
and in the blue light

from the towel-draped lamp,
I stand at your side and watch pages
float to the ground.

V. Partial Definition

*Love is of such a nature that it
changes man into the things he loves.*

—*Meister Eckhart*

Perhaps you are a carved chair,
ornate and masterfully handsome,
the dark wood rich
with use and years,

or the statue of a fierce village god
casting out evil spirits.

And you may be the colorful war masks
collected from ancient tribes,
and the sunlight of a weekday
filling your largest room.

Certainly you are the body
courting the poem
writing itself
in playful, passionate strokes.

I think you are part porcelain cat,
part Maltese song,
not yet yourself,
and not me.

VI. Forgiveness

Morning sun enlarges your bare apartment.
Plaster dust floats in the air like stars.
Boards are piled against one wall,
and trunks, and small tables, waiting.
Think how you could walk into the day
seeing your mad mother's death
as a swan, diving and swimming far
in another direction.
Only a few feathers
might be left behind;
you could pick them up,
arrange them in a vase
with a peacock plume,
or drop them out the window
to drift away.
You might descend
the five flights
to buy brioche, come back
to soak in a warm tub.
And when, as it must, night falls,
you could think of beaches, white waves rising
to meet the whiter sun,
yourself stretched on the sand, serene.
A lover might be waiting
in a nearby cottage,
dicing carrots and beef,
stirring onions in a buttery pan,
or swimming in the surf, almost
out of sight, but growing clearer
as her long strokes bring her in.

I can see you smile
as I say all this.
You'll tell me that life
is not literature,
cannot begin *in medias res.*
But I tell you, it can.

The spell of that sad old woman
can explode in sunlight.
You could wave, *Au revoir, Adieu,*
watching the fragments rise and disappear
into a sky dazzled with grace.

2

I woke last night
to see these leaves falling through the air;
and in its labor
letting its leaves fall, yellow and white,
the mind standing like a tree,
suffering its changes.

—*Mona Van Duyn*

The Room

I stumble, nearly breaking
my heel, into a wide room
lighted from the floor.
Faces are shadowed like buildings,
their rich contours etched,
the folds like blinds
at the windows.
If we look into mirrors,
we'll see our grandparents.
I too am a stranger here.

Next to me
a woman is telling a story.
She has been living
her whole adult life
here on the 17th floor.
She has no husband, no children,
but labors each day
in film. Whatever
the director wants,
she does. No, she
is no actress,
but types, carries props,
urges recalcitrant stars
to come out on time.
She has seen herself
on screen, always played
by someone else.
She likes this room,
the way plants bend down
their leaves, as if they're
listening to the couple below.

A man appears
in the doorway
carrying leaves—
whole handfuls of leaves—
the way a child
brings them in
to the first-grade teacher.
He places them
(oak and maple; it's fall)
on a long glass table.

Through the light
coming up, they're paler
than I'd have imagined,
but brilliant too,
translucent, of course,
and waxy, as if
that same child
had treated them,
making them last
a long time.
When the man
puts his hands
palms down on the table
next to the leaves,
all the veins are similar.

I walk to the window
where cardinals gather
beneath a birch.

No, no birch here—
and we're too high
for streetlamps
to show any feathers,
even deep red.
It must be reflection
from the tall
woman's dress,
its scarlet pattern,
her long white arms.

I take a drink
from a tray
being passed
by a black-suited teenager.
I choose a pale one,
not sure
what each silver-rimmed glass
contains.

In the next room
someone has switched on
a television.
Through the door

22

the screen flashes,
though the sound
is too low to hear.

For awhile
I fall asleep
on the pillows
stacked in a corner—
a blue and a red one,
another, ten-colored
and huge. They block
the light coming up
so it's easy to dream.

I wake aware
that the party
is still going on.
Hardly anyone's moved.

It's late enough now
for the sun,
that beginning dawn
diluting the light
still beating
inside.
I hear my heart.

I look into the bowl
of lilies
that seem to be growing
though their stems
have been cut
and they're held
in their places by wire.
They nod next to the wine.

The light is still rising.

Miracles

Think of it, he says, and tells me
how water from a burst pipe
spewed straight out, so far
into the startled air
it didn't harm the cupboard under it,
shelves piled high with her drawings,
lithographs, diaries,
though it came cascading
down the stairs.
He could hear it
when he put his key in the door,
the sound like his heart exploding,
imagining all her images gone.

The family sent him snapshots,
the marker of her grave
and the sculpture—
marble arms embracing a torso—
the only two objects untouched
by a blizzard piling snow
everywhere else in New Hampshire.
He points to forsythia on the hill,
unrecognizable,
but her name
blazes from gray stone.

It was a death sudden
as today's surprising snow.
In a moment the sky darkened
and then the air was white.
When the sun came out
seconds later,
nobody could believe
there'd been such change.

In a large white room
one of her plaster figures
leans forward: a woman's body
inlaid with speckled feathers,
not so much poised for flight
as seeming to watch the floor
as if it might dissolve

at her feet,
becoming sky, snow, water
she could fall through,
lifting at last
her small gray wings.

Sunday in Normandy

All afternoon strollers gather
to watch. We're on a beach
where German pillboxes
rest against hills,
some tipped on their concrete sides
like the playhouses they've become:
children's heads pop out
from the narrow blank windows
or up from behind.

A Japanese film crew
is building what looks
like a castle.
They're under a tent
forming wet sand with their hands
and with trowels
and mist they spray
from water-filled cans.

Two men carry in spires
and the sandy facade in sections.
Suddenly—it's not a chateau
but the unmistakable
Gaudi cathedral in Barcelona,
La Sagrada Familia.

They time themselves to the tide
as clouds crawl above
like ships on a steely horizon.

The cameras move closer.

A pony-tailed girl
in a pale pink suit
is unwrapped from her quilt
and placed in the background.
She's just behind the cathedral,
which is so real now
she's a delicate giant
raising one arm
in a slow, deliberate arc
toward the sun,
which does not shine.
The girl is removed.

At last the waves
reach the base of the church,

and, to the gasp of the crowd,
one breaks,
washes in through the windows
and out the front doors.
A spire begins to topple.

Gradually, gradually,
water keeps coming, taking
a tower, then a whole side.

Far away, a cathedral stands
in Spanish splendor,
a golden shell
under Southern skies.

Here, before the gray sea
with the light of Normandy
soft at its back,
it is perfectly realized,
disappearing.

The sea washes so far in
there's nothing left but a mound.
The girl disappears too,
and the crew, grown quiet,
takes down the orange tape
used to keep back the crowds,
who return to their houses
behind the banks and the bunkers.

Point of Disappearance

A young man threatens to throw himself
in front of the metro. Weaving, waving
his drunken arms in apparent rage, he yells

at the nearby *clochard,* "I don't want to be saved!"
Meanwhile, onlookers line the quai
in cautious, curious silence. A man, braver

than the rest of us, pulls him back. The boy stays
out of danger long enough to let the train come in
but is pushing the good Samaritan away

when I get on. I watch him lurching, thin
with too-quick growth and all the wrong foods,
I imagine. And I think of that age trimmed

of its myths. At times in a foolish mood
I've said I'd give up all I've learned to be 18 or 19
in Paris, forgetting then how the blood flew

through me like the runaway train I'd seen
in a film, and how the crash was always
a moment away. How the sweet machine

of the body, in perfect ease, could go days
without sleep, but the spirit darkened
quick as a full eclipse before any maze

of choices. A word could sharpen
pain to nearly unbearable grief; a smile
that felt indifferent from one who happened

into my path of attraction was a trial
I might fail, and break down in public, weeping.
Death was an alternative to everyone else's mild

acceptance of the world's devouring
loneliness. Not a few of us considered it.
But now, I read, even more of the young are leaping

from bridges, lying on tracks, their gift
to themselves mere absence
of all that emotion. I see my son lift

his head to examine his awkward presence
in a hall of mirrors. He locates
on a shimmering surface his point of disappearance.

May Day

Waiters dance on the ledge
outside my window.
They're festooning the Cluny,
my favorite café, with geraniums.

No handmade baskets with violets
seem to be left on anyone's doorstep,
but every street corner has vendors
with *muguet,* lilies of the valley
in small bouquets.

The waiters balance
like acrobats
over the sidewalk,
singing instructions back and forth,
weaving their words through rows of blossoms.

All this before the tourists stream in
for café au lait and croissants,
before stragglers from the demonstration
prop their banners in a corner like shovels,
before all but me,
here early enough to see the leaves brighten
behind wrought-iron fences
where a little museum
hides splendid unicorns, virgins
ringing a maypole, as wise beasts
watch and wink.

One of the waiters stops, lights a cigarette,
then pulls a languid hose along
like a farmer out before chores
to soak the ground for his prize roses.

Now they've tamped black earth
around each stem.
Reluctant, they climb back into the windows,
wash up, drift down the polished stairs
to their labor, almost pleased,
I like to imagine, with the stains
on their white and immaculate hands.

Marks on Paper

*Obviously letters have no "meaning" in the sense in
which words have "meaning." Letters play a merely
technical or pragmatic role in the formulation of
words.*

—*Karl Popper*

That *C* in the third line
rings like the high note
of a flute, connects
with a later *S,* almost
an echo. This is not news,
how sounds and their signs
join in the mind to make music—
but the notion of single letters,
the one *Z* the tongue lingers in,
as in a kiss, or in the grace
of *symphony,* each one moving
to its neighbor's rhythm,
and the way those isolated
notes are written, their curves
and glides on the page—
feels like the music of painting,
the way Kurosu's color bars
lead the eye to read
swells of voices.
Suggestions of ships
sail on improbable voyages
where water repeats
and faces rhyme.

The Origami Heart

Can the heart be folded like paper?
I saw it, the four corners
making four points
facing a center, the beginning
of something.
Hard to think of it flat and white,
though how it flattens and fades
is easy enough.

I am touched by the words of a man
I don't know. He heard
the woman he loves
on the phone to her other lover.
He still sees her face
as it was when he entered the room.
It stays there, like the moon
through the nearest window,
even on cloudy nights, so that when
he comes into the kitchen
he sees her again
even if she's in bed asleep.

My moon is a sliver I can't see.
It's rained all day.
But two nights ago it was crescent,
the shape of a folded wing.
Bodiless, it hovered above my dreams,
above my heart
imagining itself
a white bird sent sailing.

In Rilke's Paris

Today I wake to his meditations
on the city. While he laments
the violin next door to every
room he takes, and the men playing,
who might otherwise walk
into rivers, I listen to my neighbor
pick up his flute and trill
the morning in like an island bird.
Often jobless, he must feel despair.
But what I hear through the wall
is the low laugh of a man
who turns his back on darkness,
a woman's rippling voice, lovemaking
punctuated by song (he sometimes
sings joyous scales in the middle—
no words), and always, always,
the poet's dream—
"the winged energy of delight."

"The Anonymous Multiple Rhythm of One's Blood"

I sit on a rock, watching waves
silvered by the mercurial
Normandy sky, remembering how last night
I couldn't find my heart's wash
against any shore.
Today the heart adjusted itself
to an incoming tide in the right ear,
Mozart in the left.
Now I walk out to where,
another Sunday, I saw a cathedral
built of sand on sand.

A few white clouds
hold their own against
the gray coming down.

"Ignorant, I confront the heaven
of my life," Rilke said.

On a promontory
not far away
a figure stands, legs spread,
balanced against the wind.
Suddenly there's rain
and then no rain
and the sky is nearly blue.

Whom do we address
who once called God
to witness us
on a joyous
lonely strand?

Things I know
I cannot say,
but feel too "the same order
make the high and low tides
alternate in my blood."

What is love but this,
the light rising and falling
into us, serene
and sexless as sand.

(A cloud last night
extended, long and swollen,
into the blue,
an embarrassment
in a house
where the stirring of the blood
is other, is the sea and music.)

Another kind of love,
which embraces the world
and is not, as Rilke complained,
"an exertion."

The sky alters like a mind,
various as what touches the heart
where cathedrals are built,
unfinished, still open
to the changing light.

3

O Grandfather, look what your seed has done!
—Maxine Kumin

Traveling in the Old Country

for my mother

From Oslo we glide
through mountains gray as ash,
peaks piled with predictable snow,
and all the way down
awkward trees bent chilled
to the rain. There at the base,
an occasional red house
defies the landscape.
Mud pooled in swirls
has frozen into pattern.
"Lovely," you shudder, "but not
to live here."

As darkness settles,
the light inside grows brighter,
the outside contours
disappear into haze,
so that my photographs
(the fluorescent train light
gleaming at the margins)
will come back black and white.

Look at the woman beside us.
Her reflection in the smoky window
is yours, ten years from now—
mine too.

In a restaurant in Bergen,
beams cracked with the weight
of the roof, the old joints
unsealed by age,
you stand at an empty table
set for a dozen guests,
crystal glittering
like stars we can see
this one clear night.

For an instant
you look nearly as old as you are,
and the place, out of an Ibsen play,
seems like home, though not any
home we ever knew.
This is how I often think of you—
familiar foreign town,

room pungent with fish
and strong coffee.
Not on cozy Reuter Avenue
with my secret room
behind the built-in drawers,
and the attic
with its overflowing trunks;
not in our ranch house on the hill
surrounded by horses;
not in the little bungalow
where you live now,
defining yourself
as unexpectedly
as you consented to come here.
Back home, "up there," as you call it,
new man, new friends,
long walks in the snow,
and dancing.

In the street market I look
for lutefisk.
"Not so," you've always claimed
when I say it's soaked in lye.
But the seller nods yes,
and I grin.

Our last Norwegian meal
you order in the hotel dining room
while I bring down the bags
and check us out.
"Marinated salmon," you say
when I join you.
It comes slippery and bright
as a page of finger paint,
raw, not what you intend.
We laugh as you drink coffee
in the airport, killing
the taste.

What can we say to each other
at these moments in our lives?
Sometimes we are simply
two women who compare

the notes of generations.
Today we buy the same blouse.

You leave, beautiful now as a girl,
returning to another North.
The world rocks
as we cross seas and oceans
toward and away from ourselves.

The Will to Believe

I. Insomnia

What accounts for them—
these long nights when dreams
call me awake with their
horrors: tonight an animal
screams in its terrible
surgery, while my own legs
ache, so that I groan a little
when I turn. But this
is not great pain.
What, then?

Fear of the inner betrayals?
Age hides itself
under smooth skin,
but threatens, always,
to break from its shy reserve.

The latest: one of my two
closest high school friends,
whose breasts were the envy
of all of us.
She cupped them
in foam-rubber bras
but already, in the blue and gold
letter sweater she wore,
they were beautiful twins
the boys called the Pears
of Paradise. Now gone,
and she's having
all the therapies known
while her three sons stand guard
at her bed.

Or love?
No evidence yet to believe
on any side.
Even I, who never lie,
lie. Sometimes this seems
to be all I've learned.
Years slip by
like adolescent summers.

Night after night this darkness
gathers me up,
a baby whose days and nights
are turned around.

While the city sleeps—
even my singing, saxophone playing,
amorous neighbor—and the whole
building is quiet,
words begin their routes
out of dream,
assuming their places
as if I had only
to open the doors
to let them enter.
They are older than I,
schoolchildren
with their own schedules.
I try to follow them,
to record their progress,
room to room, class to class,
until the lessons
come clear.

Tonight my father's absence
loomed in a phrase,
and I recalled his father,
who whipped his children
mercilessly,
but sat us on his knees
like any story-grandfather,
the past a cloud
he'd slipped from under.
I think of my mother's father—
Wild West rider
in the Buffalo Bill show,
twirling a lasso
and grinning at girls,
trapper of bear and seal,
who married my mother's mother,
who didn't love him.

Sleepy at last from the pill
I finally resort to,
I imagine Grandpa Charlie
building our house,
his careful hands
framing the doors,
then back
one generation more—
Grandfather Helgeland,
who made violins.
How I wanted to play
that instrument,
sat in church
on weekday mornings
to listen to a woman practice
Mozart, and yearned
for that graceful wood
in my two small hands.

II. Elegy

How can I say this—
that the first betrayal
was his,
that he stood me on a table
saying, Jump, I'll catch you,
and when I jumped
he did,
then chastised me:
Trust nobody, he said.
Not even your father.

When Mother called to say
he would not die,
I knew the opposite,
knew in my bones,
the way his bones
would fill with disease
and in the end
how his eyes would glass over
with pain, like the eyes
of the mare we delivered
together one spring.

He brought me a playhouse—
a real log cabin,
one of the roadside cottages
that sat under shady trees
on the winding road to Chetek,
sold to make room
for a new motel.
A house of my own
for my whole childhood,
with a wide front porch
and green checked curtains
at each sunny window.

He brought home delinquent
teenaged boys
I fell in love with.
There was dark-haired Vince,
bailed out of jail,

who worked in our yard
and wouldn't go to school.
Beautiful, dangerous Vince
with the silver belt,
the boy I wasn't allowed to follow.

Years after that I helped carry hay
to the horses in winter.
I worked in our small café
where he greeted customers
with a whistle, remembering
for years who took cream
in his coffee—even strangers
who came for the summer fishing.
One cup, and he'd know forever.

He didn't come to my wedding,
such as it was—
quiet, one cold Wednesday.
Couldn't close the café,
he said.
But later gave me
the old blue Plymouth,
a box of groceries each time
we came home, and tuition,
and carried the baby happily
on his shoulder.

In Charleston,
the last year of his illness,
he could hardly sit in a car,
but seeing his first live oak
forgot the hours it took
to arrive.
While my brother sat
on a marvelous limb,
Dad put his hands on the trunk
and stood there in silence.
I thought of the trees
he'd planted,
and the ones he'd named.

When he asked to go home
for Christmas,

we bundled him into a borrowed van
that could hold a wheelchair,
and drove through town.
He wanted to see for the last time
the splendor of lights
transforming familiar streets,
making our town
a Northern heaven.
We spoke of the years
he'd climbed through snow
to string the cedars
with blue.

But after one agonized night
and day, when we stood
in a circle around his bed
while the light came and went
with the pain,
we took him back
to the hospital,
against his will,
and there, three weeks later,
he left us, as people do.

III. What We Are Given

Finally a shift
in the light
and we see
our whole lives
unroll,
a grosgrain
ribbon the stage
on which Mother
lifts us
into the air
to kiss starlight,
and Dad builds
a figure-eight
track for the new
electric train;
we play hopscotch,
thin satin chalklines
extending farther
than we can see.
There's scooting
the Model A
halfway around
the block, just
pushing the starter,
the other kids
on the running-
board—we're
driving! until
the battery's dead.
And the long walk
to the music store
to bargain
with a 50¢
allowance,
and the violin
later, in its
broken case,
under the bed,
the rosin
fragrant

as June mornings.
And longer walks,
confiding in horses
in the forbidden
fields, the lanes
leading to secret
streams where
we take off
our clothes
for the cold
spring water.
Here the future
is clotted
with trees,
thick Northern
forests
the horses refuse.
Then marriage.
Canoe trips
down the St. Croix,
sunburned and happy
on watermelon gin,
sex innocent
and unending
as the sky
blue sky it seems,
and patio coffee
talk, and building
a child's
hideaway room
as a birthday
surprise,
but finally
in dry weather,
watching the dust
lift around us
until our eyes
burn with it,
and it becomes
what we breathe.
On into middle age,
the ribbon pales

in all that sun,
tables and chairs
fading, even under
a big umbrella.
Still the colors
beneath our feet
stretch into
a distance.
Sometimes,
on windy nights,
we hear voices
traveling,
and think they
might be ours.
In sleep
our heartbeats
are the sea
breaking
and breaking
onto itself.
Shhh, we say,
this is how
we're connected.
But waking,
the meaning slips.
We think what
there is:
love,
in all its guises,
investing the world,
and the will
to believe.

From the Beginning

Lifted into the arms of the world
we feel our safety slip
as one drunken foot beneath hurls

itself out, imagines we're dancing, trips
on the rolled back, rose-swirled rug
and we almost fall. We feel the great heart skip

a beat, then speed, then clutch to hug
us closer. Too late. The baby we'll always be
knows that for years we'll tug

ourselves out of, into beds, relieved
both when there's someone there, and alone,
sure that the end of every road is grief.

Even when we travel on old cobblestone
in the carriage of childish dreams
and sometimes see our ancestors' bones

in ours, sturdy, high and refined in the cheeks,
suggesting ancient wisdom, protection
against vague dangers we fear but cannot speak

of—deep down we believe it. The election
of souls is not so far in our past.
That Presbyterian predisposition

to think of death at every turn lasts
generations. We see ourselves ablaze,
not chosen. All those years wearing masks,

and when we take them off, nobody's saved,
as far as we can tell. Or saving is something
else, but not escape. Then—we're amazed

by love, and the luminous change it brings,
the sense that this must be salvation
or its closest twin. We're ready to fling

away what we've worked for hardest, the creation
of ourselves—those children we've taught to walk
alone on narrow bridges, solve problems of addition,

perspective, and plumbing, and how to talk
to strangers—in favor of it:
Love, which overcomes the shock

of its own power. Calmed, we decide this was written
somewhere inside. Even from the beginning.